STANLEY GIBBONS

GREAT BRITAIN
NUMBERS IS
184

CONTENTS

STANLEY GIBBONS

STANLEY GIBBONS PUBLICATIONS LTD.
5 PARKSIDE, CHRISTCHURCH ROAD, RINGWOOD, HANTS. BH24 3SH

Published by **Stanley Gibbons Publication Ltd.**
Editorial, Sales Offices and Distribution Centre,
5 Parkside, Christchurch Road,
Ringwood, Hants BH24 3SH.

First published in 1975 by Birmingham and Bristol Stamp Auctions Ltd.

Typeset and printed by Pardy Printers, Ringwood, Hampshire.

This booklet lists the numbers issued for practically every stamp of Great Britain during the reigns of Queen Victoria and King Edward VII, excluding shade variations but including major colour changes and plate numbers from the 1d Black onwards. Much information is given about the numbers of stamps overprinted for the Officials, for the authorised Protective Underprints and for use in Colonial Territories.

I am very grateful to Rikki Hyde for allowing us to republish this invaluable little handbook, originally written in 1975. No serious GB collector can fail to find it of interest and some of the information which it provides is surprising to say the least!

We have retained his original text unchanged so in one or two instances there may be more copies of certain rare stamps known now than there were in 1975 but the essential information which he gave on quantities issued still provides the most comprehensive indication of relative rarities as far as early Great Britain stamps are concerned.

Hugh Jefferies
Stanley Gibbons Publications Ltd.

April 1990

ISBN 0-85259-263-9
SG Item No. 2780.

INTRODUCTION

My fortunate discovery some years ago of the rare Great Britain error of the 1883 6d on 6d, overprint double (S.G.162L), first made me think in terms of calculating rarity value from numbers issued. Just six years ago I started to compile and collate information regarding numbers issued, printed, or sold for the Victorian era, and later I extended this to the Edwardian period. This was purely for my own use, and I had no intention at that time of producing a publication. Many basic figures were first gained from the Robson Lowe Encyclopaedia, for which I express my sincere gratitude and from thereon I collated information from numerous publications, articles, and official records, all of which helped me to compile what is now an almost complete listing. My appreciation is extended to all those people whose painstaking research in these articles have helped me to produce this catalogue.

To the best of my knowledge, a combined listing dedicated to numbers issued for Victorian and Edwardian stamps of Great Britain in catalogue form has never before been published. The object of this work is to enable its users to assess rarity value and to be able to judge for themselves what is and what is not a good buy. Indeed, many amusing anomalies appear when comparing this listing with any standard priced catalogue!

The statistics in this catalogue for 'numbers issued' relate to those put into circulation, sold, or printed, whichever is the most realistic figure available. The quantities are often qualified by notes on printing spoilage or numbers officially destroyed. In some cases, where figures were not fully available, an estimated or calculated approximate number has been entered. Whilst all the quantities and data are entered in this catalogue in all good faith, I can neither guarantee their accuracy nor accept responsibility for errors.

It must be remembered that survival rate plays a large part in determining rarity. Obviously, one cannot lay down a set survival rate for every stamp, but about 2% can generally be used as a gauge for calculating possible numbers in existence for this period (say 5 to each sheet of 240). Furthermore, even the survival rate includes both mint and used examples, and generally there are at least 50 used examples for every mint copy in existence (with the exception perhaps of the 1887 Jubilee 4½. The earlier Victorian also had 240 different letter combinations to each sheet, and this should be considered by those who are attempting reconstructions. Some of the later Victorian (and a few of the earlier ones) and Edwardian were overprinted for use as 'Officials' and for use in other countries. This too should be taken into consideration, and a tabulated listing of the stamps involved and some statistical figures are given at the end of this book.

With all these points in mind, let us take an example of the sort of calculation that can be derived from this catalogue:–

Mr.X is reconstructing by letters the 1876 8d orange in used condition, and is searching for one more letter combination to complete his set. He calculates his chances of finding it as follows:–

Total number issued.................... 4,800,000		
Survival rate 2%	50)	4,800,000
i.e. divide by 50 =		96,000
Less mint survival rate 1/50th		1,920
Fraction of Letter Combination	240)	94,080
i.e. divide by 240 =		392

Mr.X would probably be looking for one of 392 copies in existence. Thus, each used 8d orange should have a letter combination rarity value of 1/392th. Let us assume for the purpose of this exercise that a unique stamp is worth £3,000 (based on the auction realisation of the 1867 10d plate 2, mint), then Mr.X should expect to pay 1/392ths of £3,000 for it (i.e. about £8). This, of course, does not take 'condition' into account, but the condition does not alter the rarity value, but only reduces the price for an inferior specimen.

When King Edward VII died on the 6th of May, 1910, Messrs. De La Rue passed over some of the printing plates to Messrs. Harrison & Sons and to the Somerset House Printers, but unfortunately from then on, it appears that inadequate records were kept of the numbers of stamps issued or produced. For this reason I regret my book finishes at 1910. However, records were kept for commemorative sets from 1924 and those issued to the end of the reign of King George VI have been listed by me, but because most specialised catalogues list the numbers sold for the Queen Elizabeth period, I feel it is pointless repeating them here.

I wish success to all the users of my book, and I dedicate this work to my beloved hobby of stamp collecting and to all those who collect the stamps of Great Britain.

BRISTOL, January 1st, 1975

Rikki C. Hyde

GENERAL INFORMATION

FORMAT

Stamps are listed in a suitable order to allow easy cross-reference with most published standard priced catalogues. Illustrations are provided for quick identification. The total number issued is given for each stamp disregarding plate numbers and this is usually followed by a more detailed break-down of the various plates and any relevant notes.

SHADES, PAPER AND VARIETIES

Most shades are caused by variation in the pigment of printers' ink and do not form separate issues. These and minor varieties of paper, watermark, gum, printing and imperforate errors of perforated issues are beyond the scope of this catalogue.

PERFORATION

The first issues from 1840 were imperforate. Line-engraved stamps of 1848 to 1858 were perforated either 14 or 16. The later line-engraved and all surface-printed issues were perforated 14 with the exception of the 1867 Maltese Cross Watermark high values. Where a perforation is not indicated in the text, it must be taken as being gauge 14.

WATERMARKS

The following are the watermarks used during the period covered:–

SMALL CROWN

LARGE CROWN

'HALFPENNY'

'V.R.'

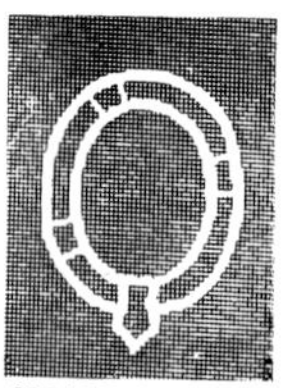
SMALL GARTER

MEDIUM GARTER

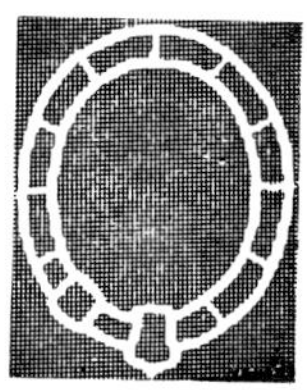
LARGE GARTER

EMBLEMS

SPRAY OF ROSE

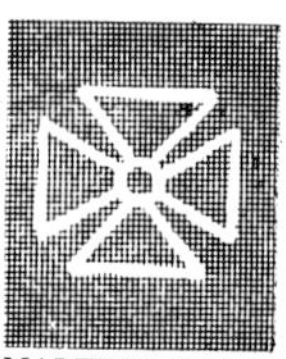
MALTESE CROSS

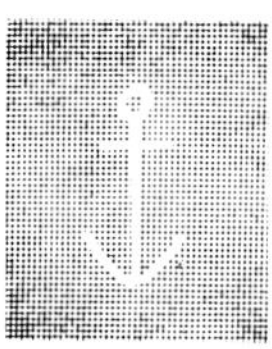
ANCHOR

LARGE ANCHOR

ORB

IMPERIAL CROWN

PLATE NUMBERS

These are listed separately for stamps which incorporate the plate number in their design, and also for the earlier 1d Blacks and 2d Blues, but not for the 1d Red 'stars' owing to their complexity.

OFFICIAL STAMPS, AND BRITISH STAMPS OVERPRINTED FOR USE IN OTHER COUNTRIES

Tabulated listing of stamps overprinted for these purposes will be found at the end of the catalogue, together with some information on numbers overprinted.

POST–1910 PERIOD

For convenience, numbers issued for commemorative sets up to the end of the reign of King George VI have been included.

ALL STAMPS WERE ISSUED IN SHEETS OF 240 UNLESS OTHERWISE STATED

QUEEN VICTORIA
Line-Engraved Issues

1840 1d BLACK *Watermark Small Crown – Imperforate*

Total number issued .... 68,158,080 (283,992 sheets)

Break-down of plates:–

Plate 1a/b	....	10,052,400	(41,885 sheets)
2	....	7,659,120	(31,913 sheets)
3	....	4,786,800	(19,945 sheets)
4	....	6,701,760	(27,924 sheets)
5	....	8,616,480	(35,902 sheets)
6	....	9,095,040	(37,896 sheets)
7	....	8,137,680	(33,907 sheets)
8	....	7,180,320	(29,918 sheets)
9	....	3,840,000	(16,000 sheets)
10	....	1,920,000	(8,000 sheets)
11	....	168,000	(700 sheets)

In addition, 8,453 sheets (2,028,720 stamps) were produced but spoilt in printing and were officially destroyed.

Notes: The total number of 1d Blacks distributed in 1840 is recorded as 63,561,840.

Owing to the deficiency of black obliterating ink for the superseding 1d Red stamps, a late consignment of black stamps was printed and delivered in January/February, 1841 which amounted to 10,018 sheets (2,404,320 stamps). This provisional printing included all plates save plates '2' and '8', whilst the scarce Plate '11' was only introduced at this stage. The above totals include this late provisional printing and of the 8,453 spoilt sheets, 182 sheets were from this printing.

1840 2d BLUE *Watermark Small Crown – Imperforate*

Total number issued .... 6,462,960 (26,929 sheets)

Break-down of plates:–

Plate 1	....	3,977.280	(16,572 sheets)
2	....	2,485,680	(10,357 sheets)

In addition, 633 sheets (151,920 stamps) were produced of the combined plates but spoilt in printing and were officially destroyed.

Notes: The total number of 2d Blues recorded as sold in 1840 is 5,382,240.

The first delivery of 2d Blues was not until 8th May, 1840 (two days after the issue of the 1d Black) and this consisted of only 600 sheets which were restricted to sale within the London area.

1841 1d RED *Watermark Small Crown – Imperforate*

Total number issued over 2,588,000,000 of which it is estimated 120,000,000 were later perforated, leaving an approximate total of imperforate stamps of 2,468,000,000.

Break-down of plates:– About four-fifths of this quantity (over 2,013,000,000 stamps) were from plates 1 to 131 of Alphabet I and the remainder (about 575,000,000 stamps) were from plates 132 to 175 of Alphabet II. Some of the latter group, i.e. Alphabet II, were later perforated (see above) and these perforated types are included in the totals for the 1854–61 issue.

Notes: The first delivery of red stamps was made by the 27th of January, 1841 and consisted of some 19,000 sheets printed from the original black plates 1, 2, 5, 8, 9, 10 and the new plate 11.

A Trial Printing of plate 11 on Dickinson silk-threaded paper was made in April, 1841 consisting of 8 sheets (1920 stamps), six sheets being gummed and two without gum.

1841 2d BLUE *Watermark Small Crown – Imperforate*

Total number issued .... about 87,960,000 (366,500 sheets)

Break-down of plates:–

Plate 3	45,960,000	(191,500 sheets)
4	42,000,000	(175,000 sheets)

Notes: The later perforated issue of plate 4 was from a new printing with the marginal inscriptions altered and not from remainders of the imperforate sheets.

1848–53 1d RED WITH "TRIAL PERFORATIONS"

Henry Archer apparently experimented on 5,000 sheets (1,200,000 stamps) with his perforating machines between 1848 to 1850, most of which were destroyed because of imperfections. A similar quantity was used by the Government in 1853 whilst making trial perforations (gauge 14 and 16) on the Napier Machine.

1854–61 PERFORATED 1D REDS

Total number issued for the combined Large and Small Crown watermarked paper perforated 14 or 16 was over 5,116,000,000 (21,316,500+ sheets). Unfortunately, figures are not available for the separate issues except that for the 1854 1d Die I on Small Crown paper perforated 16 well in excess of 410,000,000 (1,708,300+ sheets) were produced, and it is estimated that some 3,840,000,000 (16,000,000 sheets) were on white paper. Consequently, the remaining issues could only have totalled less than 866,000,000 (3,608,300 sheets) altogether.

Break-down of plates:– This varies considerably. For instance, only 19,400 sheets were printed of plate 64, whilst plate 27 produced over a million sheets on white paper alone.

1854–58 PERFORATED 2d BLUES

Total number issued for the combined Large and Small Crown watermarked paper perforated 14 or 16 was about 45,360,000 (189,000 sheets).

Break-down of plates and issues:–

Small Crown perf. 16	(plate 4)	14,160,000	(59,000 sheets)
" " 16	(plate 5)	960,000	(4,000 sheets)
" perf. 14	(plate 4)	1,680,000	(7,000 sheets)
" " 14	(plate 5)	1,920,000	(8,000 sheets)
Large Crown perf. 16	(plate 5)	960,000	(4,000 sheets)
" perf. 14	(plate 5)	15,600,000	(65,000 sheets)
" " 14	(plate 6)	8,880,000	(37,000 sheets)
Large Crown perf. 16 on white paper	(plate 6)	1,200,000	(5,000 sheets)

1858–69 1d RED WITH LETTERS IN ALL FOUR CORNERS

Watermark Large Crown – Plate Numbers printed in the design

Total number issued . . . . 13,434,000,000 (55,975,000 sheets)

Break-down of plates printed including spoilt sheets:–

Plate			Plate		
71 . .	133,680,000	(557,000 sheets)	85 . .	122,472,000	(510,300 sheets)
72 . .	125,472,000	(552,800 sheets)	86 . .	110,520,000	(460,500 sheets)
73 . .	127,176,000	(529,900 sheets)	87 . .	110,976,000	(462,400 sheets)
74 . .	127,440,000	(531,000 sheets)	88 . .	47,760,000	(199,000 sheets)
76 . .	133,320,000	(555,500 sheets)	89 . .	120,936,000	(503,900 sheets)
78 . .	147,744,000	(615,600 sheets)	90 . .	113,208,000	(471,700 sheets)
79 . .	153,264,000	(638,600 sheets)	91 . .	92,184,000	(384,100 sheets)
80 . .	118,848,000	(495,200 sheets)	92 . .	136,248,000	(567,700 sheets)
81 . .	124,872,000	(520,300 sheets)	93 . .	109,224,000	(455,100 sheets)
82 . .	63,216,000	(263,400 sheets)	94 . .	114,864,000	(478,600 sheets)
83 . .	47,904,000	(199,600 sheets)	95 . .	128,064,000	(533,600 sheets)
84 . .	88,656,000	(369,400 sheets)	96 . .	117,192,000	(488,300 sheets)
97 . .	128,832,000	(536,800 sheets)	163 . .	90,552,000	(377,300 sheets)
98 . .	84,336,000	(351,400 sheets)	164 . .	76,392,000	(318,300 sheets)
99 . .	85,272,000	(355,300 sheets)	165 . .	115,992,000	(483,300 sheets)
100 . .	61,608,000	(256,700 sheets)	166 . .	92,352,000	(384,800 sheets)
101 . .	89,400,000	(372,500 sheets)	167 . .	119,376,000	(497,400 sheets)
102 . .	118,848,000	(495,200 sheets)	168 . .	89,832,000	(374,300 sheets)
103 . .	96,144,000	(400,600 sheets)	169 . .	55,944,000	(233,100 sheets)
104 . .	42,336,000	(176,400 sheets)	170 . .	137,400,000	(572,500 sheets)
105 . .	48,624,000	(202,600 sheets)	171 . .	217,608,000	(906,700 sheets)
106 . .	93,912,000	(391,300 sheets)	172 . .	110,064,000	(458,600 sheets)
107 . .	77,040,000	(321,000 sheets)	173 . .	72,792,000	(303,300 sheets)
108 . .	51,240,000	(213,500 sheets)	174 . .	108,000,000	estimate
109 . .	56,760,000	(236,500 sheets)	175 . .	90,456,000	(376,900 sheets)
110 . .	76,032,000	(316,800 sheets)	176 . .	76,144,000	(313,100 sheets)
111 . .	108,648,000	(452,700 sheets)	177 . .	90,000,000	estimate
112 . .	71,856,000	(299,400 sheets)	178 . .	58,944,000	(245,600 sheets)
113 . .	87,840,000	(366,000 sheets)	179 . .	97,824,000	(407,600 sheets)
114 . .	55,944,000	(233,100 sheets)	180 . .	51,720,000	(215,500 sheets)
115 . .	51,360,000	(214,000 sheets)	181 . .	114,864,000	(478,600 sheets)
116 . .	84,120,000	(350,500 sheets)	182 . .	51,648,000	(215,200 sheets)
117 . .	114,960,000	(479,000 sheets)	183 . .	90,384,000	(376,600 sheets)
118 . .	105,792,000	(440,800 sheets)	184 . .	70,000,000	estimate
119 . .	118,512,000	(493,800 sheets)	185 . .	53,112,000	(221,300 sheets)
120 . .	169,632,000	(706,800 sheets)	186 . .	73,056,000	(304,400 sheets)
121 . .	97,488,000	(406,200 sheets)	187 . .	102,672,000	(427,800 sheets)
122 . .	166,416,000	(693,400 sheets)	188 . .	55,584,000	(231,600 sheets)
123 . .	107,472,000	(447,800 sheets)	189 . .	52,320,000	(218,000 sheets)
124 . .	143,448,000	(597,700 sheets)	190 . .	80,000,000	estimate
125 . .	103,128,000	(429,700 sheets)	191 . .	80,000,000	estimate
127 . .	94,872,000	(395,300 sheets)	192 . .	110,400,000	(460,000 sheets)
129 . .	104,352,000	(434,800 sheets)	193 . .	80,000,000	estimate
130 . .	98,880,000	(412,000 sheets)	194 . .	66,000,000	(275,000 sheets)
131 . .	76,968,000	(320,700 sheets)	195 . .	72,000,000	estimate
132 . .	22,872,000	(95,300 sheets)	196 . .	78,000,000	estimate
133 . .	33,936,000	(141,400 sheets)	197 . .	61,728,000	(257,200 sheets)
134 . .	190,368,000	(793,200 sheets)	198 . .	96,000,000	estimate
135 . .	45,720,000	(190,500 sheets)	199 . .	75,360,000	(314,000 sheets)
136 . .	71,880,000	(299,500 sheets)	200 . .	65,000,000	estimate
137 . .	143,088,000	(596,200 sheets)	201 . .	83,448,000	(347,700 sheets)
138 . .	168,072,000	(700,300 sheets)	202 . .	60,000,000	estimate
139 . .	46,632,000	(194,300 sheets)	203 . .	96,000,000	estimate
140 . .	235,800,000	(982,500 sheets)	204 . .	85,000,000	estimate

141 ..	43,512,000	(181,300 sheets)	205 ..	85,000,000	estimate
142 ..	50,952,000	(212,300 sheets)	206 ..	92,000,000	estimate
143 ..	68,808,000	(286,700 sheets)	207 ..	60,000,000	estimate
144 ..	49,584,000	(206,600 sheets)	208 ..	85,000,000	estimate
145 ..	130,800,000	(545,000 sheets)	209 ..	85,000,000	estimate
146 ..	110,424,000	(460,100 sheets)	210 ..	45,384,000	(189,100 sheets)
147 ..	99,192,000	(413,300 sheets)	211 ..	34,000,000	estimate
148 ..	121,872,000	(507,800 sheets)	212 ..	60,000,000	estimate
149 ..	113,976,000	(474,900 sheets)	213 ..	60,000,000	estimate
150 ..	163,800,000	(682,500 sheets)	214 ..	55,000,000	estimate
151 ..	67,872,000	(282,800 sheets)	215 ..	55,000,000	estimate
152 ..	77,496,000	(322,900 sheets)	216 ..	48,000,000	estimate
153 ..	30,816,000	(128,400 sheets)	217 ..	36,000,000	estimate
154 ..	99,624,000	(415,100 sheets)	218 ..	37,000,000	estimate
155 ..	92,472,000	(385,300 sheets)	219 ..	12,000,000	estimate
156 ..	119,232,000	(496,800 sheets)	220 ..	37,000,000	estimate
157 ..	108,000,000	(450,000 sheets)	221 ..	31,000,000	estimate
158 ..	127,440,000	(531,000 sheets)	222 ..	30,000,000	estimate
159 ..	117,528,000	(489,700 sheets)	223 ..	15,000,000	estimate
160 ..	126,000,000	(525,000 sheets)	224 ..	20,000,000	estimate
161 ..	55,752,000	(232,300 sheets)	225 ..	3,000,000	estimate
162 ..	87,648,000	(365,200 sheets)			

The total number printed for plates 71 to 225 amounted to about 14,000,000,000 stamps (58,333,000 sheets) of which some 566,000,000 stamps (2,358,000 sheets) were spoilt in printing and officially destroyed, leaving a total number actually issued of 13,434,000,000 stamps (55,975,000 sheets).

Notes: Plate '77' (together with plates 69, 70, 75, 126 and 128) was rejected owing to defects, but a few sheets were apparently printed from which seven or eight stamps have survived.

1858–69 2d BLUE WITH LETTERS IN ALL FOUR CORNERS

Watermark Large Crown – Plate Numbers printed in the design

Total number issued .... about 196,824,000 (820,100 sheets)

Break-down of plates:–

Plate 7	....	9,600,000	(40,000 sheets)
8	....	15,840,000	(66,000 sheets)
9	....	92,040,000	(383,500 sheets)
12	....	7,344,000	(30,600 sheets)
13	....	30,000,000	(125,000 sheets)
14	....	21,000,000	estimate
15	....	21,000,000	estimate

Notes: No official records were kept of numbers printed or issued for plates 14 or 15. However, accepting that these two plates are of comparable rarity, we have arrived at the above estimates by dividing equally the remainder after deducting the quantities known for the other plates from the total number issued.

1870 ½d RED

Watermark 'Halfpenny' extending over three stamps
Issued in sheets of 480

Total number issued .... 1,600,276,320 (3,333,909 sheets)

In addition, 236,923,680 (493,591 sheets) were produced but spoilt in printing and were officially destroyed.

Break-down of plates printed including spoilt sheets:–

Plate 1	....	58,320,000	(121,500 sheets)
3	....	92,400,000	(192,500 sheets)
4	....	127,008,000	(264,600 sheets)
5	....	255,936,000	(533,200 sheets)
6	....	193,008,000	(402,100 sheets)

8	....	12,500,000	estimate
9	....	2,500,000	estimate
10	....	185,328,000	(386,100 sheets)
11	....	197,280,000	(411,000 sheets)
12	....	175,000,000	estimate
13	....	175,000,000	estimate
14	....	175,000,000	estimate
15	....	80,000,000	estimate
19	....	60,000,000	estimate
20	....	48,000,000	estimate

1870 1½d RED *Watermark Large Crown*

Total number issued .... 42,638,160 (177,659 sheets)

In addition, 2,874,000 (11,975 sheets) were produced but spoilt in printing and were officially destroyed.

Break-down of plates printed including spoilt sheets:–

Plate 1 (no plate number)		15,872,160	(66,134 sheets)
3 (number 3 at sides)		29,640,000	(123,500 sheets)

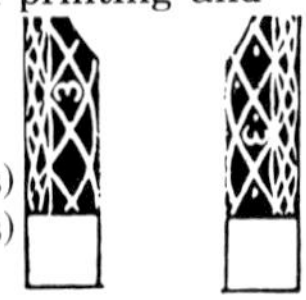

Notes: This stamp was prepared for use in 1860 but not issued and 10,000 sheets (2,400,000 stamps) of plate 1 were printed in rosy-mauve. Of these, 1,000 sheets were overprinted "Specimen" and distributed to postmasters. Of the remaining 9,000 sheets, 8,962 were destroyed in May, 1867. The remaining 38 sheets (9,120 stamps) have since been split up and are in the hands of collectors.

The error of lettering OP-PC instead of CP-PC occurred on all printings from plate 1, thus 66,134 examples (one on each sheet) were originally created. However, since the error was not discovered until 1894 many of these must have been destroyed.

Embossed Stamps

1847 1s GREEN *Paper with silk threads – Imperforate – Issued in sheets of 20*

Total number issued .... 5,655,420 (282,771 sheets)

In addition, 1,804,580 (90,229 sheets) were produced but spoilt in printing and were officially destroyed.

Break-down of Dies (estimated):–

Die I	....	3,000,000	(150,000 sheets)
Die II	....	2,655,420	(132,771 sheets)

Notes: The first printing was in 1847 when 40,000 sheets were printed. Subsequent printings were not until 1850(16,000 sheets), 1851(32,000 sheets), 1852(46,000 sheets), 1853(64,000 sheets), and the remainder were printed prior to the end of October, 1856.

1848 10d BROWN *Paper with silk threads – Imperforate – Issued in sheets of 24*

Total number issued .... 2,805,960 (116,915 sheets)

In addition, 122,040 (5,085 sheets) were produced which are believed to have been destroyed as waste, making a total printing of 122,000 sheets.

Break-down of Dies:–

Die I	....	404,016	(16,834 sheets)
Die II	....	826,104	(34,421 sheets)
Die III	....	1,382,736	(57,614 sheets)
Die IV	....	193,104	(8,046 sheets)

Notes: The first printing was in 1847 when 20,000 sheets were printed. Subsequent printings were not until 1850(8,000 sheets), 1851(16,000 sheets), 1852(14,000 sheets), 1853(32,000 sheets) 1854(32,000 sheets).

The 10d was withdrawn on August 15th, 1855 but re– issued in 1862 when 2,012 withdrawn sheets, left over at Somerset House, were put back into circulation.

1854 6d PURPLE *Watermark 'V.R.' – Imperforate – Issued in sheets of 40*

Total number issued .... 3,718,280 (92,957 sheets)

Of 6,659,920 (166,498 sheets) printed, which included 2,219,920(55,498 sheets) printed in 1856 but never issued, 2,941,640 (73,541 sheets) were apparently officially destroyed upon the introduction of the surface-printed 6d.

Notes: 4,000 of the total number issued were overprinted "Specimen" and distributed amongst various post offices.

Showing position of die number

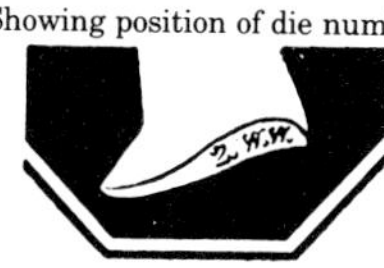

Surface-Printed Issues

1855 4d CARMINE *Watermark Small Garter – Thick, blued 'Safety' paper*

Total number issued .... 2,770,800 (11,545 sheets)

Break-down of plates:–

Plate 1	....	2,760,000	(11,500 sheets)
2	....	10,800	(45 sheets)

Notes: The quantity of plate 1 includes a late printing made in November, 1856 and January 1857 on a remainder stock of Small Garter watermarked paper which lacked the blueing giving the appearance of white paper and we estimate these amounted to 1,000 sheets. The quantity of plate 2 includes the imprimatur sheet.

4,000 stamps from plate 1 were overprinted "Specimen" and distributed amongst various post offices.

1856 4d CARMINE *Watermark Medium Garter – Thick, blued 'Safety' paper.*

Total number issued .... 1,320,000 (5,500 sheets)

Break-down of plates:– All plate 1.

1856 4d CARMINE ON WHITE PAPER *Watermark Medium Garter*

Total number issued .... 480,000 (2,000 sheets)

Break-down of plates:– All plate 1.

1856 4d ROSE *Watermark Medium Garter – Specially prepared ink*

Total number issued .... 1,800,000 (7,500 sheets)

Break-down of plates:– All plate 1.

1857 4d ROSE *Watermark Large Garter*

Total number issued .... 28,776,960 (119,904 sheets)

Break-down of plates:–

Plate 1	....	23,147,760	(96,449 sheets)
2	....	5,629,200	(23,455 sheets)

1856 6d LILAC *Watermark Emblems*

Total number issued .... 32,040,000 (133,500 sheets)

Break-down of plates:– All plate 1.

Notes: The first 2,000 sheets (480,000 stamps) were printed on azure paper.

1856 1s GREEN *Watermark Emblems*

Total number issued .... 12,120,000 (50,500 sheets)

Break-down of plates:– All plate 1.

Notes: The first 500 sheets (120,000 stamps) were printed earlier by way of an experiment on azure paper in June 1856.

1862–64 SERIES WITH 'SMALL WHITE CORNER LETTERS'
Watermark Emblems (except 4d which has Large Garter)

3d CARMINE-ROSE

Total number issued .... 5,173,200 (21,555 sheets)

Break-down of plates:–

Plate 2	....	5,172,000	(21,550 sheets)
3	....	1,200	(5 sheets)

Notes: The 3d plate 2 was first printed with a network background in the sprandrels. These were never issued and consisted of 1,458 sheets which were mainly destroyed, but a few were overprinted "Specimen" and some exist without the overprint. These are not included in the quantities given.

The 3d plate 3 were the five Registration sheets of which one or two sheets were perforated and put into circulation. A few used copies (two of which came from Yarmouth) and 2 unused examples are known to exist.

5,000 stamps from plate 2 were overprinted "Specimen" and distributed amongst various post offices.

4d RED

Total number issued .... 30,000,000 (125,000 sheets)

Break-down of plates:–

Plate 3	....	13,800,000	(57,500 sheets)
4	....	16,200,000	(67,500 sheets)

6d LILAC

Total number issued .... 15,360,000 (64,000 sheets)

Break-down of plates:–

Plate 3	....	11,040,000	(46,000 sheets)
4	....	4,320,000	(18,000 sheets)

9d BISTRE

Total number issued .... 1,573,200 (6,555 sheets)

Break-down of plates:–

Plate 2	....	1,572,000	(6,550 sheets)
3	....	1,200	(5 sheets)

Notes: The 9d plate 3 were the five Registration sheets of which some were perforated and put into circulation. About 30 used copies and 3 unused examples have been recorded.

1s GREEN

Total number issued .... 6,241,200 (26,005 sheets)

Break-down of plates:–

Plate 1 = Plate 2 . . .	6,240,000	(26,000 sheets)
Plate 2 = Plate 3 . . .	1,200	(5 sheets)

Notes: The 1s plate 2 = 3 were the five Registration sheets of which a few were unofficially perforated. 3 mint copies are known to exist.

5,000 stamps from plate 1 = 2 were overprinted "Specimen" and distributed amongst various post offices.

1865–67 SERIES WITH 'LARGE WHITE CORNER LETTERS'

Watermark Emblem (except 4d which has Large Garter)

3d ROSE

Total number issued .... 10,198,800 (42,495 sheets)

Break-down of plates:– All plate 4.

4d VERMILION

Total number issued .... 81,362,880 (339,012 sheets)

Break-down of plates:–

Plate 7	....	8,280,000	(34,500 sheets)
8	....	10,800,000	(45,000 sheets)
9	....	10,080,000	(42,000 sheets)
10	....	2,760,000	(11,500 sheets)
11	....	13,200,000	(55,000 sheets)
12	....	15,842,880	(66,012 sheets)
13	....	12,000,000	(50,000 sheets)
14	....	8,400,000	(35,000 sheets)

6d LILAC

Total number issued .... 17,760,000 (74,000 sheets)

Break-down of plates:–

Plate 5	....	14,880,000	(62,000 sheets)
6	....	2,880,000	(12,000 sheets)

9d STRAW

Total number issued .... 721,200 (3,005 sheets)

Break-down of plates:– All plate 4.

Notes: Unused copies of the unissued plate 5 exist and examples must have come from the five Registration sheets printed, from which about 3 dozen stamps from the K, L, M, & N rows were perforated by Messrs. De La Rue in 1887 for insertion in twelve souvenir albums to be presented to members of the Stamp Committee. About twenty of these stamps were later returned to the Archives and replaced in the imprimatur sheet.

10d RED-BROWN

The 10d on Emblems watermark paper was printed in error whilst preparing the 1867 issue on Spray watermark paper. Only one or two sheets could have been produced and only 10 copies have been reported of which 7 were used in Constantinople.

1s GREEN

Total number issued .... 9,362,640 (39,011 sheets)

Break-down of plates:– All plate 4.

Notes: Five Registration sheets of the 1s plate 5 with Emblems watermark were printed but never issued. Perforated examples with this watermark do not exist.

1867–80 SERIES WITH 'LARGE WHITE CORNER LETTERS'

Watermark Spray of Rose – Designs as for 1865–67 series

3d ROSE

Total number issued .... 77,280,000 (322 sheets)

Break-down of plates:–

Plate 4	....	2,641,200	(11,005 sheets)
5	....	23,158,800	(96,495 sheets)
6	....	17,880,000	(74,500 sheets)
7	....	8,400,000	(35,000 sheets)
8	....	8,400,000	(35,000 sheets)
9	....	8,400,000	(35,000 sheets)
10	....	8,400,000	(35,000 sheets)

6d LILAC (WITH HYPHEN)

Total number issued .... 14,400,000 (60,000 sheets)

Break-down of plates:– All plate 6.

Notes: The 'Board' decided on the 24th of March, 1868 that this stamp should be issued in a brighter colour and from the 22nd of July, 1868 about 22,000 sheets (5,280,000 stamps) were issued in bright violet. This quantity is included in the figure given above for the total number issued.

6d MAUVE (WITHOUT HYPHEN)

Total number issued .... 27,841,200 (116,005 sheets)

Break-down of plates:–

Plate 8	....	14,520,000	(60,500 sheets)
9	....	13,320,000	(55,500 sheets)
10	....	1,200	(5 sheets)

Notes: The 6d plate 10 were the five Registration sheets from which one or more sheets apparently got into circulation. About 5 or 6 used copies have been reported including one used on cover from Weymouth.

9d STRAW

Total number issued .... 5,315,520 (22,148 sheets)

Break-down of plates:– All plate 4.

In addition, some 1,352 sheets (324,480 stamps) were produced but officially destroyed, comprising 230,660 stamps destroyed in December, 1876 and the remainder destroyed during printing because of spoilage. A few of the sheets destroyed in December, 1876 may have come from the unissued plate 5 (see notes under the 1865–67 9d issue). The total printing of this stamp was thus 23,500 sheets.

10d RED-BROWN

Total number issued .... 3,165,540 (13,189 ($\frac{3}{4}$) sheets)

Break-down of plates:–

Plate 1	....	3,164,340	(13,184 ($\frac{3}{4}$) sheets)
2	....	1,200	(5 sheets)

In addition, 815 sheets (195,660 stamps) were produced but officially destroyed in December, 1876, making a total printing for plate 1 of 14,000 sheets.

Notes: The 10d plate 2 were the five Registration sheets which are all believed to have been perforated and put into circulation. About 30 used copies have been recorded and one mint example was discovered in 1972. Another alleged unused copy exists in the Royal Collection but this may have had a cancellation removed.

1s GREEN

Total number issued .... 48,598,800 (202,495 sheets)

Break-down of plates:–

Plate 4	....	18,480,000	(77,000 sheets)
5	....	13,318,800	(55,495 sheets)
6	....	8,400,000	(35,000 sheets)
7	....	8,400,000	(35,000 sheets)

Notes: One complete imperforate sheet of plate 4 overprinted "Specimen" has been broken up, and a single imperforate copy lettered TL has also been recorded.

2s BLUE

Total number issued .... 6,722,400 (28,010 sheets)

Break-down of plates:–

Plate 1	....	6,721,200	(28,005 sheets)
3	....	1,200	(5 sheets)

Notes: At first, plate 1 was not aligned correctly which resulted in difficulty in perforating the stamps. After 2,005 sheets were printed, Messrs. De La Rue cut the plate into separate panes and refixed them to correct the problem. However, the fault had only affected part of the sheets and since Messrs. De La Rue had invoiced 1,953 sheets prior to the correction of this plate, it is assumed that part sheets equal in quantity to 52 complete sheets (12,480 stamps) were probably spoilt and destroyed. The quantity given for plate 1 does not take this into account.

The 2s plate 3 were the five Registration sheets, some of which were perforated and put into circulation. A very few used copies are known and a mint perforated example exists in the Royal Collection.

4,000 stamps from plate 1 were overprinted "Specimen" and distributed amongst various post offices. A complete imperforate sheet overprinted as such is known, together with an imperforate single lettered NG.

2s BROWN

Total number issued .... 77,620 (equal to nearly 323½ sheets)

Break-down of plates:– All plate 1.

Notes: Originally, 1,000 sheets were printed of which after spoilage 967 full sheets and 28 half sheets were issued. After about four months the Post Office decided to discontinue this stamp and 157,820 examples (equal to over 657½ sheets) were officially destroyed. This leaves the total number put into circulation (plus a small residue of 4 sheets left over in stock) as given above. The facts indicate that about 1,000 mint copies exist.

1872 6d BUFF *Watermark Spray of Rose – Large white corner letters*

Total number issued .... 9,601,200 (40,005 sheets)

Break-down of plates:–

Plate 11 (Chestnut)	4,800,000	(20,000 sheets)
11 (Buff)	3,600,000	(15,000 sheets)
12 (Chestnut)	1,200	(5 sheets)
12 (Buff)	1,200,000	(5,000 sheets)

Notes: The five sheets of plate 12 in chestnut were Registration sheets, of which up to 4 sheets were apparently perforated and issued. A number of used examples have been recorded.

1873 6d GREY *Watermark Spray of Rose – Design as 1872 6d Buff*

Total number issued .... 7,198,800 (29,995 sheets)

Break-down of plates:– All plate 12.

1867–83 HIGH VALUES

Notes: Early printings of the stamps with Anchor watermark were on blued paper, but as printings progressed the paper became less blued and finally almost white owing to the variation in the composition of the prussate of potash. The blued and white papers are therefore really one issue and cannot be classified separately. A few of these stamps, especially those on Anchor paper, were used on telegrams.

5s ROSE *Watermark Maltese Cross – Perforation 15½ x 15 – Issued in sheets of 80*

Total number issued .... 5,480,800 (68,510 sheets)

Break-down of plates:–

Plate 1	....	3,920,000	(49,000 sheets)
2	....	1,560,400	(19,505 sheets)
4	....	400	(5 sheets)

Notes: The five sheets of plate 4 were Registration sheets and no perforated mint or used copies have yet been recorded.

5s ROSE *Watermark Large Anchor – Perforation 14 – Issued in sheets of 56*

Total number issued 537,374 (9,596 sheets)

Break-down of plates:– All plate 4.

In addition, some 404 sheets (22,626 stamps) were produced but destroyed in 1884, making a total printing of 10,000 sheets.

10s GREY-GREEN *Watermark Maltese Cross – Perforation $15\frac{1}{2}$ x 15 – Issued in sheets of 80*

Total number issued .... 242,000 (3,025 sheets)

Break-down of plates:– All plate 1.

10s GREY-GREEN *Watermark Large Anchor – Perforation 14 – Issued in sheets of 56*

Total number issued .... 224,000 (4,000 sheets)

Break-down of plates:– All plate 1.

£1 BROWN-LILAC *Watermark Maltese Cross – Perforation $15\frac{1}{2}$ x 15 – Issued in sheets of 80*

Total number issued .... 242,000 (3,025 sheets)

Break-down of plates:– All plate 1.

£1 BROWN-LILAC *Watermark Large Anchor – Perforation 14 – Issued in sheets of 56*

Total number issued .... 112,000 (2,000 sheets)

Break-down of plates:– All plate 1.

£5 ORANGE *Watermark Two Large Anchors Perforation 14 – Issued in sheets of 56*

Total number issued .... 246,826 (over $4{,}407\frac{1}{2}$ sheets)

Break-down of plates:– All plate 1.

Notes: This stamp was produced from the £5 Telegraph stamp by drilling out of each electro the word 'Telegraph' and replacing it by the word 'Postage'. It is interesting to note that only 1,500 sheets (84,000 stamps) were issued for the £5 Telegraph stamp which makes it considerably rarer than its postal counterpart.

1873–80 SERIES WITH 'LARGE COLOURED CORNER LETTERS'

2½d ROSY-MAUVE *Watermark Anchor – Issued in sheets of 192*

Notes: These stamps were printed on paper which was blued chemically and normally used for fiscal purposes. Often the blueing was so slight that it appeared absent (the so-called white paper), especially on plates 2 and 3, but on plate 1 the blueing was usually more pronounced.

Total number issued .... 17,281,920 (90,010 sheets)

Break-down of plates:–

Plate 1	....	6,720,000	(35,000 sheets)
2	....	6,720,000	(35,000 sheets)
3	....	3,840,000	(20,000 sheets)
4	....	960	(5 sheets)
5	....	960	(5 sheets)

Notes: The 2½d plates 4 and 5 on Anchor paper were printed as Registration sheets and although some of these may have been put into circulation, no mint or used perforated examples have yet been discovered.

The error of lettering LH-FL instead of LH-HL occurred on all printings from plate 2, thus 35,000 (one on each sheet) were originally created. However, since the error was not discovered until June, 1893 many of these must have been destroyed.

2½d ROSY-MAUVE *Watermark Orb – Issued in sheets of 192*

Total number issued .... 91,198,080 (474,990 sheets)

Break-down of plates:–

Plate 3	....	2,880,000	(15,000 sheets)
4	....	6,719,040	(34,995 sheets)
5	....	6,719,040	(34,995 sheets)
6	....	6,720,000	(35,000 sheets)
7	....	6,720,000	(35,000 sheets)
8	....	6,720,000	(35,000 sheets)
9	....	6,720,000	(35,000 sheets)
10	....	6,720,000	(35,000 sheets)
11	....	6,720,000	(35,000 sheets)
12	....	6,720,000	(35,000 sheets)
13	....	6,720,000	(35,000 sheets)
14	....	6,720,000	(35,000 sheets)
15	....	6,720,000	(35,000 sheets)
16	....	6,720,000	(35,000 sheets)
17	....	960,000	(5,000 sheets)

Notes: One complete imperforate sheet of plate 8 overprinted "Specimen" has been broken up.

2½d BLUE *Watermark Orb – Issued in sheets of 192*

Total number issued .... 30,720,000 (160,000 sheets)

Break-down of plates:–

Plate 17	....	5,760,000	(30,000 sheets)
18	....	6,720,000	(35,000 sheets)
19	....	11,520,000	(60,000 sheets)
20	....	6,720,000	(35,000 sheets)

Notes: There was no record kept of the quantity produced for plate 20, but the facts indicate that probably the usual 35,000 sheets were printed.

Plate 17 had already produced 5,000 sheets in rosy– mauve when the colour of this stamp was changed to blue. A further 30,000 sheets were then printed in the new blue colour, thus completing its quota of 35,000 sheets.

3d ROSE *Watermark Spray of Rose*

Total number issued .... 74,400,000 (310,000 sheets)

Break-down of plates:–

Plate 11	....	8,400,000	(35,000 sheets)
12	....	8,400,000	(35,000 sheets)
14	....	8,400,000	(35,000 sheets)
15	....	8,400,000	(35,000 sheets)
16	....	8,400,000	(35,000 sheets)
17	....	8,400,000	(35,000 sheets)
18	....	8,400,000	(35,000 sheets)
19	....	8,400,000	(35,000 sheets)
20	....	7,200,000	(30,000 sheets)

Notes: Plate 13 was defective and no stamps were printed from it.

It is possible that five Registration sheets were printed from plate 21 on Spray of Rose watermarked paper, since an imprimatur sheet does exist. However, no mint or used perforated examples have yet been discovered.

4d VERMILION *Watermark Large Garter*

Total number issued .... 3,601,200 (15,005 sheets)

Break-down of plates:–

Plate 15	....	3,600,000	(15,000 sheets)
16	....	1,200	(5 sheets)

Notes: The 4d plate 16 were the five Registration sheets, but at least two of these sheets were perforated and issued. Some 8 used copies have been reported, but no mint perforated examples have yet been found.

4d SAGE-GREEN *Watermark Large Garter*

Total number issued .... 12,000,000 (50,000 sheets)

Break-down of plates:–

Plate 15	....	4,800,000	(20,000 sheets)
16	....	7,198,800	(29,995 sheets)
17	....	1,200	(5 sheets)

Notes: The 4d plate 17 were the five Registration sheets from which two sheets are believed to have been perforated and issued. A very few used copies are known to exist, mostly emanating from Bradford, but no mint perforated examples have yet been found.

One complete imperforate sheet of plate 15 overprinted "Specimen" has been broken up.

4d GREY-BROWN *Watermark Large Garter*

Total number issued .... about 2,350,800 (9,795 sheets)

Break-down of plates:– All plate 17.

6d BUFF *Watermark Spray of Rose*

Total number issued .... 1,200 (5 sheets)

Break-down of plates:– All plate 13

Notes: These were actually Registration sheets which were apparently all perforated and issued. About 18 used copies have been recorded, mostly used at Leeds, but no mint examples have yet been found.

6d GREY *Watermark Spray of Rose*

Total number issued .... 37,198,800 (154,995 sheets)

Break-down of plates:–

Plate 13	....	8,398,800	(34,995 sheets)
14	....	8,400,000	(35,000 sheets)
15	....	8,400,000	(35,000 sheets)
16	....	8,400,000	(35,000 sheets)
17	....	3,600,000	(15,000 sheets)

Notes: One complete imperforate sheet of plate 16 overprinted "Specimen" has been broken up.

8d ORANGE *Watermark Large Garter*

Total number issued .... 4,801,200 (20,005 sheets)

Break-down of plates:–

Plate 1	....	4,800,000	(20,000 sheets)
2	....	1,200	(5 sheets)

Notes: The 8d plate 2 were the five Registration sheets. No mint or used copies of these have yet been discovered.

8d PURPLE-BROWN *Watermark Large Garter*

This stamp was prepared for use in July, 1876, but not issued and about 10,000 sheets of plate 1 were printed of which most were officially destroyed. However, a few mint copies have survived. This stamp was eventually issued in orange (see above).

1s GREEN *Watermark Spray of Rose*

Total number issued .... 48,001,200 (200,005 sheets)

Break-down of plates:–

Plate 8	....	8,400,000	(35,000 sheets)
9	....	8,400,000	(35,000 sheets)
10	....	8,400,000	(35,000 sheets)
11	....	8,400,000	(35,000 sheets)
12	....	8,400,000	(35,000 sheets)
13	....	6,000,000	(25,000 sheets)
14	....	1,200	(5 sheets)

Notes: The 1s plate 14 were the five Registration sheets from which possibly only one sheet was perforated and issued. Four used copies are known, mostly emanating from Greenock, but no mint perforated examples have yet been found.

1s ORANGE-BROWN *Watermark Spray of Rose*

Total number issued .... 1,200,000 (5,000 sheets)

Break-down of plates:– All plate 13.

Notes: No record was kept of the production of this stamp, but since there was no longer a great demand for a 1s value owing to the introduction of a Telegraph stamp of the same duty, it may be safely assumed that there was only the one creation warrant, for 5,000 sheets, made out in September, 1880.

POSTAGE STAMPS USED ON TELEGRAMS

When the Government took over the private Telegraph Companies in 1870, telegraph charges were mainly defrayed by the use of an embossed 1s stamp similar in appearance to the embossed 1s postage stamp of 1847, but the charges could also be paid by using ordinary postage stamps. Early in 1876 the Post Office introduced special telegraph stamps and the use of postage stamps was no longer permissible. On the 1st of November, 1881 telegraph stamps were abolished altogether and from then on all telegrams were prepaid by the use of ordinary postage stamps. Consequently, certain post–1881 values (especially the 1s denomination) had a considerable telegraphic usage and most of the stamps used on telegrams were eventually officially destroyed. In this catalogue the proportions and quantities quoted of postage stamps most frequently used for telegraphic purposes are calculated by comparing such denominations with the numbers sold of the official telegraph stamps issued prior to 1881. The use of the telegraph system started to decline after 1900 owing to the increasing use of the telephone.

1880–83 SERIES WITH 'LARGE COLOURED CORNER LETTERS'

Watermark Imperial Crown – Designs as in 1873–80 series

Notes: The quantities produced from each plate in this series are not recorded, but some information is available on the total numbers sold for each value. The total quantities must therefore be taken as approximate and the break-down of plates have been estimated.

2½d BLUE

Total number issued	92,640,000	(386,000 sheets)
Break-down of plates:–		
Plate 21	30,240,000	(126,000 sheets)
22	31,200,000	(130,000 sheets)
23	31,200,000	(130,000 sheets)

3d ROSE

Total number issued	45,900,000	(191,250 sheets)
Break-down of plates:–		
Plate 20	15,900,000	(66,250 sheets)
21	30,000,000	(125,000 sheets)

Note: At least one quarter of these stamps were used on telegrams.

4d GREY-BROWN

Total number issued	13,248,000	(55,200 sheets)
Break-down of plates:–		
Plate 17	6,048,000	(25,200 sheets)
18	7,200,000	(30,000 sheets)

6d GREY

Total number issued	30,000,000	(125,000 sheets)
Break-down of plates:–		
Plate 17	13,200,000	(55,000 sheets)
18	16,800,000	(70,000 sheets)

Notes: When the 6d on 6d lilac was introduced in 1883 the remaining stock of plate 18 in grey was overprinted "I.R.Official" and these are included in the above total.

It is estimated that some 1,750,000 stamps from plate 17 and 1,250,000 stamps from plate 18 were used on telegrams.

1s ORANGE-BROWN

Total number issued .... 59,520,000 (248,000 sheets)

Break-down of plates:–

Plate 13	....	31,920,000	(133,000 sheets)
14	....	27,600,000	(115,000 sheets)

Notes: At least one half of these stamps were used on telegrams.

'3d' SURCHARGED IN CARMINE ON 3d LILAC

Total number issued .... 14,400,000 (60,000 sheets)

Break-down of plates:– All plate 21.

Notes: At least one quarter of these stamps were used on telegrams, and a few were used for revenue purposes.

'6d' SURCHARGED IN CARMINE ON 6d LILAC

Total number issued .... 9,600,000 (40,000 sheets)

Break-down of plates:– All plate 18.

Notes: One example of this stamp exists with a double overprint and this was discovered by the author of this book in 1966.

At least one quarter of these stamps were used on telegrams, and a few were used for revenue purposes.

1880–81 NEW DESIGNS 'WITHOUT PLATE NUMBERS'

Watermark Imperial Crown – No check letters (except for 1d value)

½d GREEN

Total number issued .... 902,520,000 (3,760,500 sheets)

1d VENETIAN RED

Total number issued .... 1,462,584,000 (6,094,100 sheets)

1½d VENETIAN RED

Total number issued .... 49,248,000 (205,200 sheets)

2d ROSE

Total number issued .... 27,396,000 (114,150 sheets)

Notes: One imperforate copy overprinted "Specimen" has been recorded.

5d INDIGO

Total number issued .... 9,804,000 (40,850 sheets)

Notes: One imperforate copy overprinted "Specimen" has been recorded.

POSTAGE STAMPS USED FOR REVENUE PURPOSES

With the introduction of the 1881 1d lilac, penny postage stamps could also be used for revenue purposes and the words "Postage & Revenue" were incorporated in the stamp design. In February, 1883 this inscription and usage was extended to all other values up to 2s.6d. The main demand for revenue usage at that time was for the 1d, 3d, 6d, 1s, and 2s.6d. denominations.

THE PARCEL POST

The Post Office introduced the Parcel Post on the 1st of August, 1883 and thus stamps used after that date may be found with parcel post obliterations. Since 3d was the minimum inland parcel post rate, values of 3d and over were mainly used.

1881 1d LILAC *Watermark Imperial Crown – No check letters in corners.*

Total number issued .... 34,095,984,000 (142,066,600 sheets)

Break-down of Dies:–

Die I (14 dots in each corner)...	495,984,000	(2,066,600 sheets)
Die II (16 dots in each corner)..	33,600,000,000	(140,000,000 sheets)

Notes: It is estimated that about 1% of these were used for revenue purposes.

1883–84 HIGH VALUES *Watermark Large Anchor – Issued in sheets of 112*

Notes: At first this issue was printed on paper blued for revenue purposes, but early in 1884 the blued paper was replaced by white paper. The actual quantities printed on blued paper are not available, although considerably less were produced than on the later white paper. The totals given below are therefore of the combined printings on blued and white paper. A few of these stamps were used on telegrams

2s.6d LILAC

Total number issued .... 10,325,392 (92,191 sheets)

Notes: A few of these stamps were used for revenue purposes.

5s ROSE

Total number issued .... 7,520,800 (67,150 sheets)

Notes: These stamps may be found perforated 12 but they were never issued and originate from parts of waste sheets sent to Somerset House for official reasons.

10s ULTRAMARINE

Total number issued .... 1,929,200 (17,225 sheets)

1884 £1 BROWN-LILAC

Watermark three Imperial Crowns – Issued in sheets of 80

Total number issued .... 360,160 (4,502 sheets)

Notes: A few of these stamps were used on telegrams.

1888 £1 BROWN-LILAC

Watermark three Orbs – Issued in sheets of 80 – Design as 1884 £1

Total number issued .... 80,800 (1,010 sheets)

Notes: This issue was actually an error of printing on fiscal paper. When the error was discovered the Post Office withdrew the remainder which had not already been circulated (probably some 10,000 stamps of the above total) and overprinted them "I.R. Official" for official use.

A few of these stamps were used on telegrams.

1883–84 UNIFIED SERIES

Watermark Imperial Crown – Check letters in corners

Notes: All the following values (except the 9d) may be found imperforate or perforated 12. These were never issued and came from parts of waste sheets sent to Somerset House for official purposes.

½d SLATE BLUE *Design as 1880–81 ½d*

Total number issued .... 949,920,000 (3,958,000 sheets)

1½d LILAC

Total number issued .... 57,240,000 (238,500 sheets)

2d LILAC

Total number issued .... 27,240,000 (113,500 sheets)

2½d LILAC

Total number issued .... 111,960,000 (466,500 sheets)

3d LILAC

Total number issued .... 42,480,000 (177,000 sheets)

Notes: At least one third of these stamps were used on telegrams or for revenue purposes.

4d DULL GREEN

Total number issued .... 15,960,000 (66,500 sheets)

5d DULL GREEN *Design as 1½d*

Total number issued .... 12,000,000 (50,000 sheets)

Note: There were two Dies of the 5d of which only Die II was issued and represented in the above total. Die I (with a short line under 'd' of value instead of a dot) was prepared and some 2,500 sheets printed, but the plate cracked early in use and most of those already printed were officially destroyed, although a few mint copies are known to have survived.

6d DULL GREEN *Design as 2d*

Total number issued .... 21,240,000 (88,500 sheets)

Notes: At least one third of these stamps were used on telegrams or for revenue purposes.

9d DULL GREEN *Design as 2½d*

Total number issued .... 6,480,000 (27,000 sheets)

1s DULL GREEN *Design as 3d*

Total number issued .... 54,000,000 (225,000 sheets)

Notes: At least four fifths of these stamps were used on telegrams or for revenue purposes.

1887–1900 "JUBILEE" ISSUE

Watermark Imperial Crown (£1 three Crowns)

½d VERMILION

Total number issued .... 13,494,216,720 (56,225,903 sheets)

½d BLUE-GREEN

Total number issued .... 2,605,146,600 (10,854,777 sheets)

1½d PURPLE AND GREEN

Total number issued .... 492,960,000 (2,054,000 sheets)

2d GREEN AND CARMINE

Total number issued .... 305,448,000 (1,272,700 sheets)

2½d PURPLE ON BLUE PAPER

Total number issued .... 469,920,000 (1,958,000 sheets)

Notes: One sheet printed on the gummed side was found at Southampton in 1904.

3d PURPLE ON YELLOW PAPER

Total number issued .... 527,040,000 (2,196,000 sheets)

Notes: It is estimated that about 45,000,000 of these stamps were used on telegrams or for revenue purposes.

4d GREEN AND BROWN *Issued in sheets of 80*

Total number issued .... 222,000,000 (2,775,000 sheets)

4½d GREEN AND CARMINE *Issued in sheets of 80*

Total number issued .... 82,000,000 (1,025,000 sheets)

Notes: This value was introduced in 1892 for use on parcels weighing two pounds, but in June, 1897 this rate became obsolete and a large stock of 4½d stamps remained unused. For this reason the 4½d is more common mint than used and the majority of used copies are, of course, parcel cancelled.

5d DULL PURPLE AND BLUE

Total number issued .... 142,800,000 (595,000 sheets)

Notes: Two Duty Plates exist of the 5d value, of which probably some 100,000 sheets were of Duty Plate Iand the rest Duty Plate II.

6d PURPLE ON RED PAPER

Total number issued .... 784,800,000 (3,270,000 sheets)

Note: It is estimated that about 75,000,000 of these stamps were used on telegrams or for revenue purposes.

9d PURPLE AND BLUE *Issued in sheets of 80*

Total number issued .... 77,920,000 (974,000 sheets)

Notes: It is estimated that about 7,000,000 of these stamps were used on telegrams or for revenue purposes.

10d PURPLE AND RED *Issued in sheets of 96*

Total number issued .... 33,465,600 (348,600 sheets)

1s GREEN

Total number issued .... 138,600,000 (577,500 sheets)

Notes: It is estimated that over 100,000,000 of these stamps were used on telegrams or for revenue purposes.

1s GREEN AND CARMINE

Total number issued .... 27,996,000 (116,650 sheets)

Notes: One sheet with inverted watermark was found at Liverpool in 1900.

Very few of these stamps were used on telegrams, as the basic telegraph rate was changed from 1s to 6d in 1899, and this stamp was issued in 1900.

£1 GREEN *Issued in sheets of 80 – Design as 1884 £1*

Total number issued .... 701,760 (8,772 sheets)

Notes: A few of these stamps were used on telegrams.

KING EDWARD VII

1902–10 DE LA RUE PRINTINGS

Watermark Imperial Crown (½ to 1s); Large Anchor (2s.6d to 10s); three Crowns (£1)

½d GREEN

Total number issued .... 18,524,101,680 (77,183,757 sheets)

Notes: 67,101,600 (279,590 sheets) of the above total were produced in special sheets of 240, half with inverted watermark, for use in Post Office Booklets.

1d RED

Total number issued .... 19,012,289,520 (79,227,837 sheets)

Notes: 103,524,960 (431,354 sheets) of the above total were produced in special sheets of 240, half with inverted watermark, for use in Post Office Booklets.

1½d PURPLE AND GREEN

Total number issued .... 297,518,400 (1,239,660 sheets)

2d GREEN AND CARMINE

Total number issued .... 287,701,440 (1,198,756 sheets)

2½d BLUE

Total number issued .... 603,649,200 (2,515,205 sheets)

3d PURPLE ON YELLOW PAPER

Total number issued .... 468,448,800 (1,951,870 sheets)

4d GREEN AND BROWN

Total number issued .... 312,208,080 (1,300,867 sheets)

4d ORANGE

Total number issued .... 96,727,200 (403,030 sheets)

5d DULL PURPLE AND BLUE

Total number issued .... 191,848,800 (799,370 sheets)

6d PURPLE

Total number issued .... 561,474,240 (2,339,476 sheets)

Notes: It is estimated that about 120,000,000 of these stamps were used on telegrams or for revenue purposes.

7d GREY

Total number issued .... 5,963,040 (24,846 sheets)

9d PURPLE AND BLUE *Issued in sheets of 80*

Total number issued .... 51,010,560 (637,632 sheets)

10d PURPLE AND RED *Issued in sheets of 96*

Total number issued .... 33,465,600 (348,600 sheets)

1s GREEN AND CARMINE

Total number issued .... 125,063,280 (521,097 sheets)

2s. 6d PURPLE *Issued in sheets of 56*

Total number issued .... 9,634,464 (172,044 sheets)

5s CARMINE *Issued in sheets of 56*

Total number issued .... 4,343,472 (77,562 sheets)

10s BLUE *Issued in sheets of 56*

Total number issued .... 1,513,680 (27,030 sheets)

£1 GREEN *Issued in sheets of 40*

Total number issued .... 804,880 (20,122 sheets)

1910 PREPARED FOR USE BUT NOT ISSUED – 2d TYRIAN PLUM

It was intended that this stamp should have been issued on the 6th of May, 1910, but on that day the King died and practically all the stamps printed were officially destroyed. The few surviving copies include a complete sheet (except that one corner stamp is missing) owned by the General Post Office, a mint pair in the Royal Collection and some ten other known examples. One of these stamps was used on a letter to the Prince of Wales (later King Georve V) on the 5th of May, 1910 and this is housed in the Royal Collection.

King Edward VII died on the 6th of May 1910 and although further provisional stamps bearing the King's portrait were produced between 1911 and 1913 by Messrs. Harrison & Sons and the Somerset House Printers, these were actually issued during the reign of King Georve V.

Following the King's death, Messrs. De La Rue handed over some of the printing plates to Messrs. Harrison & Sons and to the Somerset House Printers for printing the provisional issues and Messrs. De La Rue's contract for printing stamps ended on the 31st of December, 1910. Unfortunately, the new printers kept inadequate records of numbers of stamps printed and the Post Office Record Book ceased recording quantities at the end of 1908. Therefore, it is impracticable to supply numbers of definitive stamps issued after 1910.

The numbers issued or printed for commemorative sets up to modern times are known. Since most specialised catalogues record the quantities issued for the Queen Elizabeth period, it is pointless repeating them here, but for easy reference details are given for the commemorative sets issued until the end of the reign of King George VI.

1924/25 BRITISH EMPIRE EXHIBITION: All values combined (17,000,000)

1929 POSTAL UNION CONGRESS: ½d(677,500,000), 1d(341,000,000), 1½d(751,250,000), 2½d(26,750,000), £1(61,000)

1935 SILVER JUBILEE: ½d(353,400,000), 1d(150,400,000), 1½d(490,000,000), 2½d(14,200,000)

1937 CORONATION: 1½d(388,731,000)

1940 POSTAL CENTENARY: ½d(82,896,960), 1d(232,903,680) 1½d(40,412,800), 2d(121,065,120), 2½d(312,957,440), 3d(22,128,000)

1946 VICTORY: 2½d(307,832,500), 3d(43,085,700)

1948 ROYAL SILVER WEDDING: 2½d(147,500,000), £1(419,628)

1948 CHANNEL ISLANDS LIBERATION: 1d(5,934,000), 2½d(5,398,000)

1948 OLYMPIC GAMES: 2½d(155,350,000), 3d(32,554,000), 6d(24,397,000), 1s(32,187,000)

1949 UNIVERSAL POSTAL UNION: 2½d(135,150,000), 3d(16,450,000) 6d(11,450,000), 1s(11,400,000)

1951 FESTIVAL OF BRITAIN: 2½d(260,142,000), 4d(22,197,000)

THE OFFICIALS

1840 V.R. 1d BLACK *Watermark Small Crown – Imperforate – Letters "V.R." in upper corners*

It was intended to issue this stamp with the first postage stamps of 1840 but although it was prepared for use and some 5,000 sheets were printed, it was never officially released. However, used copies on covers are known and these probably passed through the post in error. Some were also used for trials of obliterating inks and cancelled with a red Maltese Cross or a concentric ring experimental obliteration. Many of the unused copies in existence probably came from post office circulars which were distributed on the 7th of May, 1840 and to each of which two of these stamps were attached. It is recorded that 3,302 sheets of the V.R. 1d Black were officially destroyed on the 25th of January, 1843, leaving a residue of 1,698 sheets or 407,520 stamps which could be in collectors' hands.

GREAT BRITAIN STAMPS OVERPRINTED FOR OFFICIAL USE

From 1882 to 1904 various Government departments overprinted stamps which were then current, for official use. These overprints consisted of "I.R. Official" (Inland Revenue), "O.W. Official" (Office of Works, "Army Official", "Govt. Parcels" (Government Parcels), "Board of Education", "R.H. Official (Royal Household), and "Admiralty Official". The stamps overprinted were as follows:–

1880–83	6d grey (plate 18), 1s orange-brown (plates 13 and 14).
1880–81	½d green.
1881	1d lilac.
1883–84	5s rose, 10s ultramarine.
1884	£1 brown-lilac watermark Crowns.
1888	£1 brown-lilac watermark Orbs.
1883–84	½d slate-blue, 1½d lilac, 2½d lilac, 6d dull green, 9d dull green, 1s dull green.
1887–1900	Jubilee all values except 3d and 4d, including the colour changes.
1902–10	Edward all values except the two 4d's, 7d and 2s6d. The ½d was only overprinted on the blue-green shade.

It has not been possible to compile a complete listing of the numbers of stamps overprinted for official purposes, but set out below is the information that is so far known.

INLAND REVENUE

1901 6d purple on red paper (1887–1900 issue) .... 120,000 (500 sheets)

1901 1s green and carmine (1887–1900 issue) .... 2,400 (10 sheets)

1904 6d purple (1902–10 issue) .... 248 copies are known of which 6 are used and 242 are mint. Most of the used examples are postmarked May 14th, 1904 and the mint includes a near complete sheet of 234 housed in the Post Office archives, a marginal pair and a single in the Royal Collection, and a block of four in the National Museum of Ireland at Dublin.

1902 10s blue (1902–10 issue) .... The Post Office archives holds 51 mint copies. Others exist.

1902 £1 green (1902–10 issue) .... The Post Office archives holds 35 mint copies. Others exist.

OFFICE OF WORKS

1901 ½d blue-green (1887–1900 issue) .... 6,000 (25 sheets)

1902 5d dull purple and blue (1887–1900 issue)......... 12,000 (50 sheets) 949 were used

1902 10d purple and red (1887–1900 issue)..........800 (10 sheets of 80) 480 were used.

1903 10d purple and red (1902–10 issue) .... 240 (1,440 were printed in 15 sheets of 96, but 1,200 were officially destroyed. 134 were used.

ARMY OFFICIAL

1903 6d purple (1902–10 issue)................. Number printed 480,000(2,000 sheets).

The bulk of this printing was officially destroyed.

GOVERNMENT PARCELS

1897 1d lilac "overprint inverted" error....................... 240 (1 sheet)

Notes: This is the only recorded instance of an inverted overprint on a British stamp for use in Great Britain.

1900 1s green and carmine (1887–1900)...................... 36,000 (150 sheets)

BOARD OF EDUCATION

1902 5d dull purple and blue (1887–1900 issue)............................ 5,520
(66,000 were printed, 60,480 were officially destroyed)

1902 1s green and carmine (1887–1900 issue)............................ 2,400
(33,000 were printed, 30,600 were officially destroyed)

1902–04 5d dull purple and blue and 1s green and carmine (1902–10 issue) ....
The majority of these two values were destroyed on the 14th of May 1904 when the general issue of the Officials ceased. The 1s was never officially issued. Very few of the 5d were issued. However, one or two of the 1s were used by some high official and a very few of the 5d were also used. The Post Office archives holds 114 mint copies of the 1s value.

ROYAL HOUSEHOLD

No information available.

ADMIRALTY OFFICIAL

No information available.

GREAT BRITAIN STAMPS OVERPRINTED FOR USE IN OTHER COUNTRIES

Although prior to 1880 British stamps had been used in many countries apart from Great Britain, Cyprus was the only country to actually overprint the stamps with the name of their country. During the 1880's this practice was adopted by six other countries (i.e. Bechuanaland, British East Africa, British Levant, Mafeking, Oil Rivers Protectorate, and Zululand), and in 1907 Morocco Agencies also began overprinting British stamps. Most of the British Levant stamps were only surcharged with a new currency and it was not until 1905 that they overprinted the stamps 'Levant'. In later years other countries have overprinted Great Britain stamps, but the information given below is confined to the period covered by this book 1840 to 1910. The stamps of Great Britain overprinted by the various countries were as follows:–

1858–69 1d Red (plates 174, 181, 184, 193, 196, 201, 205, 208, 215, 216, 217, 218 and 220).

1870 ½d Red (plates 12, 15 and 19).

1873–80 2½d rosy-mauve (plates 14 and 15), 4d sage– green (plate 16), 6d grey (plate 16), 1s green (plate 13).

1881 1d lilac

1883–84 2s.6d lilac, 5s rose.

1883–84 2½d lilac, 5d dull green.

1887–1900 Jubilee all values to 1s except 1½d, 4½d, and 1s green and carmine.

1902–10 Edward all values to 10/– except 7d and 9d.

Unfortunately, the totals of the stamps so overprinted are not known for all the countries, but the information that is available is indicated below.

BECHUANALAND

1881 1d lilac	*Numbers not known*
1887–1900 Jubilee ½d vermilion, ½d blue-green, 2d, 3d, 4d, 6d, 1s green	
1902–10 Edward ½d(blue-green and yellow-green), 1d, 2½d	

BRITISH EAST AFRICA

1881 1d. lilac	1,440	(6 sheets)
1887–1900 Jubilee 2d	1,440	(6 sheets)
5d	780	(3 sheets)

BRITISH LEVANT

1883–84 2s.6d lilac	*Number not known*
1883–84 2½d lilac, 5d dull green	*Numbers not known*
1887–1900 Jubilee ½d vermilion	6,000 (25 sheets)
2½d, 5d, 10d	*Numbers not known*
1902–10 Edward all values (including both 4d colours) except 7d, 9d, 10s and £1	*Numbers not known*

CYPRUS

1858–69 1d Red (plates 174, 181, 184, 193, 196, 201, 205, 208, 215, 216, 217, 218 and 220)	total about 480,000	(2,000 sheets)
1870 ½d Red (plates 12, 15 and 19)	total 68,640	(143 sheets of 480)
1873–80 2½d rosy-mauve (plates 14 and 15)	total 319,584	(1,664½ sheets of 192)
4d sage-green (plate 16)	13,440	(56 sheets)
6d grey (plate 16)	3,360	(14 sheets)
1s green (plate 13)	2,880	(12 sheets)

MAFEKING

1881 1d lilac		3,600	(15 sheets)
1887–1900 Jubilee ½d	vermilion	6,000	(25 sheets)
2d		2,400	(10 sheets)
3d		1,440	(6 sheets)
4d		2,320	(29 sheets of 80)
6d		1,680	(7 sheets)
1s	green	570	(2⅜ sheets)

MOROCCO AGENCIES

1902–10 Edward all values (including both 4d colours) except 3d, 7d, 9d and £1. The ½d was only overprinted on the yellow-green shade .... *Numbers not known*

OIL RIVERS PROTECTORATE

1881 1d lilac		33,360	(278 half sheets)
1887–1900 Jubilee ½d	vermilion	33,600	(280 half sheets)
2d		33,480	(279 half sheets)
2½d		57,000	(475 half sheets)
5d		33,540	(279 half sheets + one ¼ sheet)
1s	green	6,720	(56 half sheets)

ZULULAND *Numbers sold*

1881 1d lilac		459,776	(1,915+ sheets)
1883–84 5s rose		998	(nearly 9 sheets of 112)
1887–1900 Jubilee ½d	vermilion	268,224	(1,117+ sheets)
2d		31,987	(133+ sheets)
2½d		28,544	(118+ sheets)
3d		11,949	(49+ sheets)
4d		20,250	(253+ sheets of 80)
5d		6,428	(26+ sheets)
6d		11,405	(47+ sheets)
9d		3,701	(46+ sheets of 80)
1s	green	4,654	(19+ sheets)

PROTECTIVE UNDERPRINTS

The following quantities of line-engraved stamps were officially underprinted (under the gum) by Messrs. Perkins, Bacon & Co. for the various companies in the period November, 1872 to the end of 1877. It must be remembered, that in addition to those listed some were officially and unofficially both underprinted (under and over the gum) and overprinted before and after this period by Messrs. Perkins, Bacon & Co. and by the private firms using them, whilst Messrs. De La Rue officially underprinted certain surface– printed issues.

OXFORD UNION SOCIETY (O.U.S.)

1d Red .... 420,720 (1,753 sheets)

J. & C. BOYD & CO.

1d	Red	696,000	(2,900 sheets)

W.H. SMITH AND SON

1d	Red	96,000	(400 sheets)
2d	Blue	12,000	(50 sheets)

COPESTAKE, MOOR, CRAMPTON & CO

½d	Red	1,968,000	(4,100 sheets of 480)
1d	Red	1,374,720	(5,728 sheets)
1½d	Red	76,080	(317 sheets)
2d	Blue	144,000	(600 sheets)

GREAT EASTERN RAILWAY (G.E.R.)

1d	Red	360,000	(1,500 sheets)

Notes: Note: This comprises the whole of the printing for the Great Eastern Railway, whose stamps were underprinted between November, 1873 and January, 1877.

PROTECTIVE UNDERPRINTS

O.U.S.

J. & C. BOYD & CO. 7 FRIDAY ST.

W. H. SMITH AND SON, 186, STRAND.

COPESTAKE, MOORE, CRAMPTON, & CO., London.

COPESTAKE, MOORE CRAMPTON & CO. LONDON.

G. E. R.

A SUMMARY OF THE NUMBERS OF ADHESIVE POSTAGE STAMPS ISSUED DURING THE REIGN OF QUEEN VICTORIA

The following numbers of adhesive postage stamps were issued in the period 1840 to 1900:–

	Stamps	*Sheets of Stamps*
½d	19,552,079,640	78,133,089
1d	56,644,726,080	236,019,525
1½d	642,086,160	2,675,359
2d	696,690,960	2,902,879
2½d	813,720,000	3,535,500
3d	796,872,000	3,320,300
4d	415,670,640	3,581,961
4½d	82,000,000	1,025,000
5d	164,604,000	685,850
6d	1,010,759,480	4,288,962
8d	4,801,200	20,005
9d	92,009,920	1,032,708
10d	35,843,500	503,505
1s	411,295,260	1,972,937
2s	6,800,020	28,333
2s.6d	10,325,392	92,191
5s	13,538,974	145,256
10s	2,395,200	24,250
£1	1,496,720	19,309
£5	246,826	4,408
Totals	81,397,961,972	340,011,327

When Messrs. Perkins, Bacon & Co. finally completed their printing contracts for the Line-Engraved series on the 31st of December 1879, the Board of Trade stated that the numbers of line-engraved stamps produced by the firm (excluding wastage) were:–

½d	1,600,276,320
1d	20,699,858,040
1½d	42,638,160
2d	338,540,280